MINDS OF MIND

POEMS ABOUT LIFE AND LIFELESS

IRENDU BHARDWAJ

Contents

Contents

Contents

Preface

This book is written for everyone who finds themselves different and seek the differenece between the misery and the reality. This Anthology has been combined with mostly artistic,questioning, philosophical, and optimistic poetry. Also talking about the genres of the poems written is diverse and also depends on the diversification made by the readers themselves. An Artistic approach towards life, question the misery happening, psyche the people dwell, are some of the common adherence inked around the book. I personally as the author of the book would like to make the readers think upon the facts, as I believe understanding is different for different readers and everyone got there own stories to dwell an relate.

Talking about the references made in the book makes it very interactive with its readers. Which makes them think upon various phenomenas happening to us and all around. The main interest lies on making the readers realize about the Art and analogy of mind.

WorD lAvA

All these years I waited for revolution
Until I discovered I am the revolution

NuClEaR wEaPoN

You might be embracing the light,
Just make sure It is your own.

I

POETRY

It is unique from person to person,
For various reasons and features.
Like a drug or abstraction,
Binding the readers and pleasers.

Two faces, readers and pleasers,
They dive to find and inculcate.
For war, for love and listeners,
To live again, to incarnate.

Counting figures and silent roars,
Poetry, making life livable.
Like a medicine or cure,
For the wounds not visible.

It can be someones rage,
Those who are vulnerable.
Trapped in the mental cage,
Who find the world unstable.

&

What poetry sustains?
Just incidents and tragedies.
To overcome what drains,
To mature our maturity.

&

So, the more we read,
The more we ride out,
The less to keep in mind,
The less to weep about.

&

InK

II

LETTER OF A FAMILY MAN

Once I was a family man,
With a heart full of love.
Had a life with a plan
And a son like dove.

Everything that concerned.
All that was done.
Every penny I earned,
They were the reason.

&

Smiles, tears, pain and pleasure.
Every feeling was well framed.
A hero, a loser sometimes,
I was in various roles for them.

&

Part, where journey took a turn,
I lost my half part forever.
With no coming back,
In a better place somewhere.

ᙚ

Things were changing,
And the bond we owned.
I was sixty-something,
And he was twenty-one.

ᙚ

This was the time,
He must have shown.
But the dove flew away,
He was now grow.

ᙚ

Here being so subtle,
I try my best all alone.
Left to cry and cuddle,
Myself on my own.

ᙚ

My body and my story,
Cremated under the cold land.
I manifest remembering,
Once I was a family man.

tHe OtHeR pArT

SoMeWhErE

III
MY SELVES

I have often seen
One of my selves,
That keeps me alive
And lets me dwell.

&

Not the one forgotten,
Willingly years ago.
To bear this life,
To lose all control.

&

Accompanied by knowledge,
And full of conscience.
Being rare to average,
With no self-reliance.

I witnessed my deflections,
Discovered my scars.
And lost my perfections,
In this imperfect war.

The lower self,
My passionate lover.
Your love is poisonous,
Never lets me sober.

Takes my pain,
And trauma together.
Like an illusion,
Just not forever.

For my two or more faces,
Of my heart and my mind.
My higher self is numb,
For a moment of time.

IV

VISION

What we see through,
Behind the curtains
Of lavishness and slough.
In snowfalls and rains.

An ordinary work of art,
Something beyond further.
Which developed and stuck,
Made you an observer.

Halting with the sunrise,
Beginning with the sunset.
This nocturnal mind,
Is tied with this fate.

Is this a bane?
To scrutinize more.
Being so sane, and
Away from the shore.

৪৩

A sacrifice or murder.
Nicely buried humans,
Dead animals scattered,
Turning into humus.

৪৩

Humorous or lame,
Always been a prodigy.
The view is rigid to explain,
When compared to reality.

৪৩

A sinner or a saint,
Expounding wrong and right.
Apart from curses and blames,
Embracing alone and quiet.

৪৩

Death into life,
Life over salvation.
Depends on your sight,
Depends on your vision.

৪৩

rEaLiSe = ReAl EyEs

DaY oR nIgHt ?

V

JUDGEMENT DAY

When the judgment day arrives,
You get surrounded by faces.
Childhood, youth, family
Flashes of many phases.

Money, memories and relations,
Nothing left to keep.
You have lived a dream,
And now you can sleep.

The body stabilized,
Not being able to move.
You find yourself,
The one watching you.

Beloved ones mourn,
With tears and sorrow
Or they may fear,
It is their turn tomorrow.

જી

Screaming all names,
For a thousand times.
Now too late to call them,
As they cannot mind.

જી

Melting part by part,
Entities of every part survive.
All these decades passed,
Was this the life?

જી

This world is a stage,
We all are clowns.
With different roles and rage,
In ups and downs.

જી

And at the end
Every soul, fair or dark.
An evil or a saint,
Gets back to their start.

The judgment day,
A story well framed.
Reoccurring to us,
Till salvation is attained.

UnBeAtAbLe

VI
REALIST

I see skeletons,
All around no humans.
Sound of the void,
That no one listens.

Nothing is dark,not even light
My eyes know each colour.
None I see no wrong or right
And no judgements to fear.

Soul means different here,
For me and my sphere.
Bizarre system we adhere,
Away from the common share.

Money is the most powerful,
To get the most powerful things,
But peace of the mind,
Comes with no earnings.

ॐ

A crime may be justified,
As a crime to everyone.
What put the one to do it,
Not that bothers to anyone.

ॐ

Sowing to cut more trees,
To show what we built.
It is same as rasing childrens,
To get them killed.

ॐ

Sound like a dominant,
I act not the dumb.
And play what I am,
There is nothing topretend.

VII
IT CAN'T BE GOD

You have seen it,
Or felt it atleast.
If it makes darkness lit,
And you find peace.

&

But views never ally,
Of different gods or the one.
What opposites and athiests,
Try hard to learn.

&

It guides to live,
In all stands of life.
Will meet us after the end,
Like a hollow surprise.

Who says to eat well and drink,
Who says to be more human.
But consume everything,
Everthing on earth except humans.

&

Show love to animals,
Not when you eat them.
Differ your love,
When you treat them.

&

There is heaven and hell,
Waiting for us withstand.
Wrongs and rights we did,
Which were part of his plan.

&

Prayers and pleasings,
From all of us.
For breathing and blessing.
We keep our blind trust.

&

A contradictry balance
Who we all should fear
Who gives us the wounds
And stands with the cure.

If there is the only one,
In so many roles.
While various roles,
Even divides million souls.

It cannot be God,
If its too manly to sound.
In this misery so far,
God waits to be found.

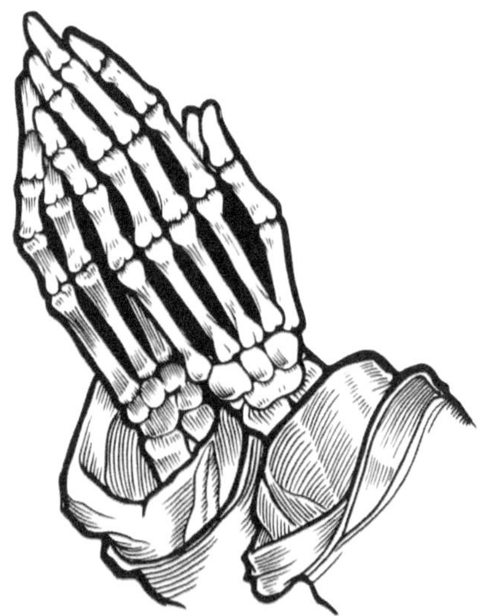

SaViOuR

VIII

ALONE

Scrutinize yourself,
Your angels and demons.
The lines you made,
For no specific reasons.

To heal in exile,
To define your fate.
Once in a while,
To recover and reincarnate.

You could be alone,
With a bunch of people.
The mentality you own,
Is uncultured and dull.

But there could be someone
Breathing and bearing like you,
Awaiting and so numb,
Suffocating to go through.

You are self-driven for life time,
Life is just a phase.
In which you are alone,
For a reason to embrace.

HuStLeR

IX

DO NOT LOVE

Do not love,
Feelings which prolong.
Bury some of them,
There is nothing wrong.

Do not love,
When you are not yourself.
When drunk or dumb,
In search of wild to dwell.

Do not love,
If you are lame.
Too commonly polite,
Filled with fear and vain.

To do not love,
To invade or rustle.

To act brighter,
To sound hustle.

❧

Do not love,
For god's sake.
Until you witness
The one with no face.

❧

Do not love,
If you are the only one
Loving absurdly making it
Sophisticated and curved.

❧

Do not love
If you are emotionally reamed
And enough unloved,
Waiting to be seemed.

X

OLD EYES

Those old eyes,
The ones who are aged.
Fed up and full of life,
With some free thoughts caged.

So, It took years to grow,
Out of the ones who left.
Death climbed each of them,
Memomries of faces are kept.

Too many scenes seen,
Enthusiatic and mournings.
But the eyes never felt,
It just carried the feelings.

A lot of people,
A lot to see within them.
Now times have come,
Eyes don't judge anyone.

৪৩

Windows of the soul,
That watched , that listened.
To something never told,
Always confesssed, never spoken.

৪৩

Many lives started,
Many lives gone.
These eyes reacted,
To abstracts and wrongs.

৪৩

Misery is hidden,
Hidden in those old eyes.
Illusion and Images,
Till the day they die.

XI

ARTISTS ALL AROUND

Movements of the wheels,
Delineating static roads.
Converged dusts of summer,
Rains that made trees bowed.

Street lights raising,
Flames under frames.
Those people sleeping,
On the walking lanes.

A drunk feeding a cat,
Many drunks in a bar.
The cigar that burnt,
Those lips as scars.

Only man at the bus stop,
Forbidding the night.
Who lost his job,
Still not lost might.

And there is a dog,
Similar to me.
Living every thought,
In the present,undoubtedly.

Soil shaped into senses,
References of mind.
Strokes unprecedented,
Of paintings lost in time.

Image of the images,
Art behind the clowns.
All I can observe
Artists all around.

XII

MANIFEST

Extract yourself,
If you are alive.
Not dead and buried,
Just left out by life.

Convey yourself,
If you are rare
Or too common
And hard to adhere.

Reveal yourself.
In wrangles and dreams
When lost in your best,
Without any mean.

Indicate yourself.
In slow hands of clock,
Of this fast moving world
Of stresses and shocks.

ॐ

Express yourself.
In arts and rags,
Something you hate,
Or love to have.

ॐ

Intimate yourself.
In self obsession,
Self occupied and devoted,
To reflect discretion.

ॐ

Manifest yourself.
If you do not,
You might lose to
Embrace what you got.

XIII
WRONG ERA

In an unearthly earth,
With a lot diversity.
He dreams of a birth,
In the pre-history.

When life was not puzzled,
With enough precision.
In absence of rustle,
For profaned reasons.

When God do existed
Among the ambiance.
Like a non-hedonist,
Without crowns and lance.

When Glimpses of the universe,
Mirrored the night sky.
Somewhere in the vast desert,
Values and valuables buried inside.

જ

Why does he feel,
So much for ancient times.
Though he would never get,
What is left long behind.

જ

There is an impulse,
To struggle, to survive.
Not to attain death,
Just to be enough alive.

જ

Inconsolably dying,
Among this fetish aura.
He finds himself living,
In a wrong era.

XIV
ILLUSION OR LIFE

Neither it connate.
Nor it is going to end.
We live it so wide awake,
But we live it to pretend.

&

A hoax way of living,
So reliable and true.
We never bothered to see,
What was always within the loops.

&

Roles we chose,
Identical to a mind.
No selfness enclosed,
Being one of the other kinds.

An expedition of hate,
Redemption of rage or rush.
Having equal fate,
For love and lust.

ॐ

We may realize this,
With our real eyes.
It could be late,
Maybe after demise.

ॐ

All that money earned,
And respect gathered.
When the sides turned,
Nothing left to be mattered.

ॐ

A life barely cultivated,
With passion and premonition.
All the misery created,
Is just an illusion.

XV
INTROVERT

Watching this world
Without the eyes.
Sitting next to ourselves
Without any ties.

Faces had come and gone.
Phases had come and gone.
We stood still with
Timidity of our own.

Not much to speak
Never the less to write.
We skipped the days,
And slowed the nights.

Escaping social circles
And flaunts of mankind
We all non-verbal, kept
Expressing in our mind.

&

Self absorbed and obsessed,
And looking mentally weak.
With a lot of thoughts messed,
Being so natural and meek.

&

When did exactly
You become the modest.
Far from the reality,
Close to your closet.

&

Whatever be the chances,
Destiny is the same.
Being so reserved
Demands no change.

&

Since the age of eight or nine
You found everything absurd.
And understood the hymn
No company is fine for an introvert.

DiFfErEnt OnE

XVI

UNBOTHERED BOOK

It was a book,
Abandoned among others.
Soulfully appealing to look
At its intimating features.

&

Like a shaded body,
On which a lot written.
By those lunatics who
Desires to be listened.

&

Some confessions framed,
And love stories by
The teenage gems,
Embracing the sweet lie.

&

Some pages wrecked,
By fans and fanatics.
Making it unveil,
And cozily retractive.

Drawings and doodles,
With ink, sometimes blood.
Figures of friendship,
And of broken hearts.

A book of art for sure,
Published and rewritten.
With so many starts
For so many ends.

Just stacks of pages,
Less understood.
Adorned by begetters,
An unbothered book.

XVII
STRATIFIED

Suffused with inner traits,
Still not found.
The true extractor,
Of our realest form.

It is hard to tell,
The decisions we make.
Are all by our self,
With no one's stake.

Different faces to wear,
On different occasions.
That traces joy and fear,
For the attire chosen.

Sometimes we hate,
Our own reflection.
Which makes a damage,
And dents to relations.

ಬಿ

A skin for society,
To cover the inner rustle.
For hiding all anxiety,
And breathing struggle.

ಬಿ

A layer that we made,
For friends and family.
One for the self,
To fake the reality.

ಬಿ

The way we all are living,
And then leaving from here.
We might never be truly,
Unbiased and not layered.

XVIII
NARCISCTIC LOVERS

There are always people around,
And they love to love them.
Even though love is not found,
They love being among them.

For things and thrills,
For trying out feelings.
To have some worth,
Even if they worth nothing.

For things and thrills,

Because they have been alone,
Unbothered for a long time.
No one bothered these clowns,
As they burn to throw shine.

With their own rules,
Which they let all us choose.
Just keep them soulful,
Use much you want to use.

FoOl ThEm

XIX

REALITY

Travelling through ages,
In infinite roles.
Different opinions and cases,
Still its existence is bold.

May be not god,
Or his preacher.
A myth, evolved
To be more unclear.

Away from conscience,
Away from insanity
With no characteristics,
Life span and quality.

In particles and particulars,
Far than cosmos and galaxies.
Over time and dimensions,
There exists reality.

***

DiMeNsIoNs

XX

STUDYING WITH THE POETS

Not speaking much,
Rather preferring the papers.
To create worlds,
Loops and mind makers.

Carrying times of ages,
And a mind to slow it.
In books and novels,
We sow it and grow it.

Lost in the wars of
Writers and mortality.
And even worse in
Stories of tragedies.

Something to fight.
To write, to weep about.
That no one could defeat,
Still keeps it throughout.

ॐ

Every day is a chaos,
This puts us down.
Fissuring the soul,
Making clowns out of clowns.

ॐ

Resonating Sufis and trances,
In a numb zone.
Not taking any chances,
Of not being alone.

ॐ

In my lower self,
In the highest part of it.
A believer of art lives,
Studying with the poets.

XXI

BIBLIOPHILE

The people of the words,
The people who are crooked.
Somtimes alone on their own,
Also alone in a group.

A book addict tends,
Addictions of the stories.
Of poems and incidents,
Of future and the past burried.

The one who are stuck in here,
Who are running somwhere else.
Away from the atmosphere,
As the characters they dwell.

To think upon, to relate.
What has been written,
What we concieve,
Through the feelings given.

৵

They read people's look,
It is in their reflex.
To grab and shook,
To fit in and adjust.

৵

So every book reader,
Is a book on its own.
The more they are explicit,
The less they have shown.

৵

wOrLd

XXII

LONG LOST RETURNS

One of those homecomings,
Bringing happiness and sorrow.
They waited for this happening,
Since ages, for this tommorow.

જી

It is a rebirth on same earth,
Around same good things.
After abusing more than the worth,
And then only regrets clings.

જી

Everything is almost alright,
Now that they are united.
To understand and hold tight,
For the years not sighted.

જી

Hungry for love and light,
The dark mind kept going.
Away from people in disguise,
Who inherits no showing.

෧ර

There lies the family,
Much from which is taken.
As you went trough tragedy,
But now you are awaken.

෧ර

Real faces and real phases,
Nothing to extract.
A son is born again,
A brother is back.

෧ර

DoVe

XXIII

ATHEISM

We are psychological
Outcomes of evolution.
So afraid of death,
We created thy illusion.

Religious peace, nefarious peace.
Traditions and customs are,
Pieces of a piece.
Misinterpreted from the start.

There is something existing,
And that is you.
Not the one inversely living,
The one spiritually true.

A believer of believes,
Accept the attire they conceive.
God or godliness,
Nothing to achieve.

Just have to embrace,
The inner case well.
And you can create
Your heaven and hell.

MiSeRy

XXIV

BIZARRE

More hard work,
For more features.
To stuck with the luck,
What happened to us.

More hard work,
For more features.
To stuck with the luck,
What happened to us.

&

Be busy, busy enough
To hide the reality.
It is so easy to be tough
With this wicked mentality.

&

To lapse the time,
Of days into years.
While creating memories,
For the mirrors.

We have lost ourselves,
Somewhere nearby.
When we taught ourselves,
To abandon our fears.

&

To live for the world,
Which is already existing.
Unaware, unbothered about
Our reasons of existence.

&

Filled with love and
A lot of sorrow.
Questing lusts with no believe
Of seeing tomorrow.

&

Acceptance for drowning,
Instead of dying.
Laughing and lying,
And tired of crying.

&

We are scars of the moon,
Gazing the stars.
In simple hierarchy of living,
We all are so bizarre.

GeNeRiC

XXV
KILLING AN ARTIST

It was not easy
To offend my soul.
For so many times,
For so many roles.

To listen to music,
Without any feel.
And not to relate to,
What you conceal.

Blinded eyes of mine,
Imaging darkness all inside
Even though there is a shine,
I lack the sight.

There is no sleep,
With this peculiar emptiness.
When the urge fights,
And fights back for oneness.

❧

Impossibly neglecting,
All acts of art.
And ceasing my brain,
To respond to the heart.

❧

When you have to breathe,
For being alive.
For being human,
To ignite and elite.

❧

Words of insight on reams,
Just to write, not to insist.
It was Death of dreams,
And Killing of an artist.

XXVI
CONMAN

When I am not me,
Fragmented and thrived.
When there is nothing to see,
And to go through this strive.

I'm a mirror escaping
Reflections and reality.
Inverted and accusing
Beauty and hostility.

I'm a song usually played
Towards morning.
By sleepless heads,
Who keep on mourning.

I'm same as a bird flying,
High in the sky.
So high and flaunting,
But plumps for land to die.

I'm a train carrying,
Passengers of various mentalities.
Speaking different accents,
Assorted by tragedy.

I'm an ocean shore,
Crafted by waves.
Turning glasses into gems,
With no amaze.

I'm a poem written half,
Partially in longhand.
And left unconcerned,
Unread and withstand.

I'm a burning pyre,
Sustaining nothing.
Burning peacefully,
For the beginning.

When I am not me,
Regardless of my self
My humanity and span.
I live phases like a conman.

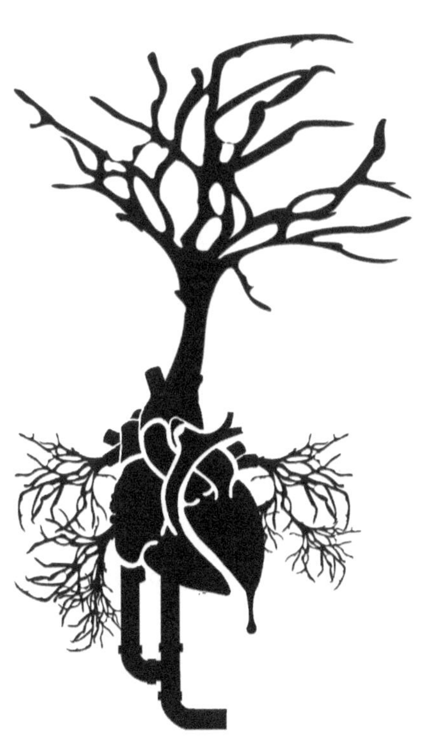

RoLeS

XXVII
DAY DREAMING

A disease for the diseased,
An escaper's mentality.
To pass day after day,
They think, they think the reality.

There is always thinking,
No essense of outcomes.
Nothing new happening,
No way to overcome.

A life with him or her,
Better days or a better phase.
The festish for the future,
Ruining the present always.

This needs to be done today,
That will be done tommorow.
No shame in failing everyday,
There is always time to borrow.

But tommorow never comes,
As it is always the now.
Tables never turns,
If no efforts are allowed.

It is good to be a dreamer,
To imagine the most deep.
It is all good only when,
Your achieve what you seek.

DrEaMeR

DoEr

XXVIII
CHILDHOOD

When the mind was still
Unfilled with guilt.
And was unneutered,
With less emotions built.

Growing with the hunger,
And quench that kills.
Inflated adrenaline or anger,
Discovered these feels?

When smalls things
Meant big deals.
An imaginary friend,
We made and concealed.

When the sun
Reached to us late
Even we slept early
Unlike sleepless wide awake.

&

Glowing with fuss
Pampered and chastised.
During sick days,
And for miserable fights.

&

When we feared
Not life, but calculations
Sober and unclouded
Away from revolutions.

&

When we had
Few screens around.
And more faces
To talk and bound.

&

When we actually
Loved the rain.
Dampened and drenched
Alike through window frames.

Where did it go
Concluded or lost.
We stand in the present
Childhood gazes from the past.

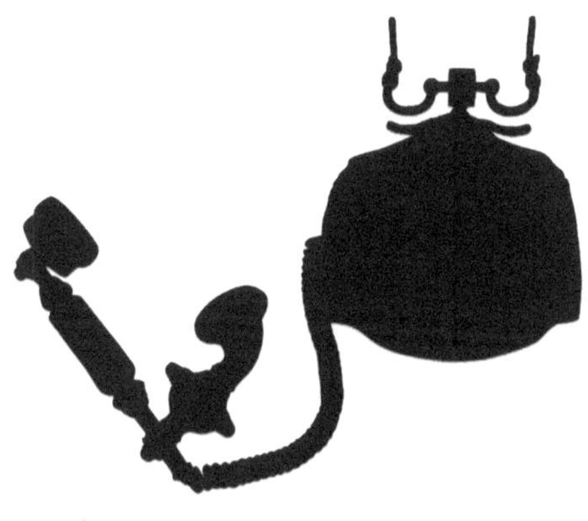

PaSt

XXIX

NEVER ENOUGH

Just a last hit before the heat,
That makes you a burning coal.
Just one last time to feel it,
One last breath before turning old.

A lot more money,
Before we collapse.
To lapse the reality,
To seize the steps back.

A lot of pleasure,
Before surviving pain.
But not much to measure,
To make us Insane.

Our actions and aspects,
Showings and stuff.
Hunger or addiction it is!
Nothing is never enough.

LiTtLe MoRe

XXX

IMMORAL SIDE

There is an immoral man,
Tied with my mind.
Who talks to me and
Makes me blind.

Provokes to lose my self,
In the worldly drama.
Which is full of adrenaline,
And full of trauma.

He loops different places,
Phases and time.
He hides his faces,
Behind that psychic smile.

Needs to attain a love,
That barely happened.
And wants to kill this body,
With heart full of dents.

ॐ

To be obsessed,
With this lunatic voice.
Or to posses it,
Is always our choice.

ॐ

We all are immoral,
Victims and culprits.
It just depends,
How much we embrace it.

ॐ

Soulfully at some verge
My soul cries.
This is an immortal urge,
That never dies.

ॐ

With all of my strength
And hope of being right.
It ends with our end
Unaccepted immoral side.

SinNer

XXXI
KINDS OF PEOPLE

A kind of people,
Abandoned and aside.
Searching lost temples,
And cathedrals to hide.

There is a kind of people,
Cracks and maniacs.
Who don't sleep the whole night,
Whose generic vitals lacks.

A kind of people,
Who never cry or shiver.
Who mourns for years,
Or may be forever.

There is a kind of people,
Who can eat alone.
And entertain themselves,
With company of none.

&

A kind of people,
Who are unloved and stiff.
And left to realize
What wrong they did?

&

There is a kind of people,
Lost from the present.
Who adores the past
And cannot pretend.

&

A kind of people,
Who hope to see someone.
Even after long gaps or
Decades have summed.

&

There is a kind of people,
They don't drink ever.
So much sober and toned,
But psychedelic by nature.

Kinds of people,
And their kinds of tales.
To read them,
To write and prevail.

CrOwd

XXXII

CANCEROUS

Ribs are meant for melting,
With this scar inside.
Breaking every breath of mine,
In the dark with no light.

Now that I want my wants,
Not to be wanted by anyone.
To take this far away,
To break it like a stone.

The pain in the tissues,
Is enough to use,
And increase the doses,
To erase all issues.

After all this time,
It has grown much .
To be clearly visible,
In your tone and touch.

❧

To feel just fine,
But the smile gets carved,
Even the reason behind
Is a poisonous art.

❧

The best could be done,
Just do not care.
What has developed inside,
Some disease or a layer.

❧

Just live the life,
And shine bright.
Feeling the days,
Left to fight.

❧

XXXIII
WRITER'S BLOCK

In need of competence,
And visions full of mist.
Loud speaking silences,
Slanting a deaf artist.

All characters chocked,
Dead for a while.
Escaped from here instead,
For some time in exile.

Figures of speech and
Plots coming bright.
But they oppose reality
So, you do not write.

It's like you breathe
And cannot exhale
The more you try to focus
The more you fail.

A blocked mind
With flashing scenes
Every dream you find
Is already seen.

There is nothing to feel
Nothing to attain
Neither immense zeal
Nor trivial pain.

Behind the illusions
Words got linked.
I wrote every notion
Just not with the ink.

XXXIV
TWO CORPSES

You can see them often,
When you have lost someone.
Carrying on your shoulders,
Step by step towards them.

Passing the blue sky,
And beneath the concrete roads
And they spot you
With glitter to uphold.

There is lot less to admire,
And a lot more to realize.
In their godly attire and
In those small watery eyes.

No great theories to embark,
Common stories to recite.
They mess with the dead,
As they don't feel alive.

&

So many skulls smashed,
By those skillful hands.
For begetting salvation,
Not to be left withstand.

&

Every morning starts
With mourning, till dusk.
And this chasing lasts,
With eternal hush.

&

There are two corpses,
One on the pyre.
Other who has burnt
All his desires.

XXXV

STAND BY YOURSELF

There are enough portrayals,
And depictions of betrayals.
If you are the one,
Who stays in no one's tale.

So calm and vital,
Willing to move ahead.
If you are a suicidal,
But not dead yet.

All the days of midnight,
The thoughts of rebel.
If you cry hard inside,
But your eyes don't tell.

If you loved so hard,
Not expecting the same.
If you have a heart,
You would love again.

₭

If you don't stop
Creating myths and fates.
If you are retarded,
Not precluded yet.

₭

Less human, more savage.
Full of belligerence.
If you are not average
And feel the difference.

₭

The urge to be thrown,
Recklessly deserted.
If you are alone
But not introverted.

₭

You felt for that person,
Or carved by someone else.
If you fall on your own
Stand by yourself.

tRapPed

ಙ

AnGeL

XXXVI

ORDINARY PEOPLE

There may be more universes,
And galaxies to discover.
More depth in sciences,
Advancements to conquer.

Great theories to prove,
Many arts to embrace.
A lot luxury to use,
To enhance more taste.

Some people don't care,
Who merely survive
Limited days on this sphere,
Without any strive.

Living in the reality
For the smallest of things.
With their big hearted mentality,
And fear for the sins.

છ

They are so busy in work,
For food and future.
Their family and luck,
This is all they got to adhere.

છ

All efforts and thoughts,
In the direction they lead.
They still pray to god,
For basic needs and deeds.

છ

They are unordinary people,
Living an ordinary life.
To escape from this hell,
For heaven above the skies.

XXXVII

DEAD DREAMING

Every time I close my eyes,
To reach that bond.
To the place it drives,
Where I don't belong.

Immobilized body of mine,
Thrown away so far.
Without any rites,
Adorned with the scars.

Symphonies of the mind,
All emphasized here.
And the demons of mine,
Are no more in there.

Nothing to intend,
Numbness to elite.
I would end like this,
Between dead and alive.

&

May be for thy self,
In the wildest of valleys.
Or embodying the
Darkest of bodies.

&

Somewhere alone,
Abandoned and lost.
Not on a pyre,
Thrown like a corpse.

&

Dream of my death,
Challenges versatility.
I wish to forget that
Before the reality.

XXXVIII
UNVEIL

Try not to die,
Let it pour and bleed.
Like a fabric dyed,
Let it burn instead.

You want to hustle
For the intense art.
Differ yourself from people,
Differ from their heart.

Do not prison your emotions,
Behind the societal bars.
The faces you have chosen,
Over your alluring scars.

There must be a key,
To your rusty locks.
That begs you with plea,
That makes you self-talk.

❦

It made you change,
Thrilled or amused.
It was some slang,
That someone abused.

❦

Something that you hide,
From your head to heel.
Every raging strives,
Inside that you feel.

❦

So let them read you,
Like a mythical tale.
You want to be artistic,
There is nothing to veil.

XXXIX

THE ANSWER SEEKER

It has not been a year,
Feels like I know you for years.
Since a lot can lapse year by year,
I have been on my own with this fear.

It fears me all the time,
I am the one running out of time.
To take out the best of me,
But I keep breaking after each line.

So there must be an answer,
Give it a thougt straight.
Should I even try more,
To carry this ahead?

ImAgInArY

XL

TIME LAPSE

Preconscious of the one,
Mesmerized with chaos.
May be since childhood,
Existed, this unnatural force.

Acts that we did,
Out of the personality.
Facts that we hid,
Knowing the reality.

What caused the stand?
A person or an incident.
Made you lost and
Absent from the present.

Tragedy unluckily
Happens to the one.
Who are traumatized,
For so many reasons.

ॐ

If there is guilt,
For being yourself.
Surviving this disaster,
Without any help.

ॐ

Which is hard to carry on,
Devastated from luck.
As the world moves,
You are the one stuck.

ॐ

The mind has gapped,
Which we couldn't mind.
All these years lapsed
At the wrong time.

XLI

I CANNOT WRITE

I cannot write,
What I don't realize.
Through my eyes,
Within my sight.

When voices of the head,
Are too cloudy.
Echoing to jot down,
Every misfortune proudly.

I cannot write,
When I feel no pain.
Prosperous and bright,
Without any guilt or shame.

Everyone is veiled,
Within covers and layered.
People and their tales,
Nothing is purely fair.

I cannot write
Each time I want to.
So much of strive,
Never satisfied though.

pLeAsUre

XLII

INSIDE YOU

What is inside you,
Got different meanings.
Depends on your choices,
And mindful thinking.

Virtuous or evil,
That is up to you.
You are the one,
To define it too.

Is it something
That exits or not.
Or it is just a myth,
An airy thought.

Carried it throughout,
And nobody knew.
Your complex, your type
Could be false or true.

❧

As different people got
Much different insiders.
For some it is dark,
For some it is brighter.

❧

It might be the mighty
That guides you.
It may be satanic,
That fights you.

❧

What we conceive
Within our roots.
The part you believe
Is exactly inside you.

XLIII

DRUNK AND DUMB

A strange feeling,
Of being lost forever.
In hope for leaning,
And never getting sober.

Euphoria hits so hard,
Of every memory we miss.
Which hates to retard,
And loves to risk.

Euphoria hits so hard,

The venom of curiosity,
Dazes and amazes you.
And roots this mentality,
That the world chases you.

Gloomy glow of the face,
Paleness in the eyes.
The trance in your walk,
Unveiling your disguise.

ॐ

Impressions of situations,
Felonies flashing wide.
To numb your emotions,
To lose this fight.

ॐ

Drunk and dumb,
Appealing the same.
Out of your senses,
Just weak and lame.

SaMe InSaNe

XLIV
PHENOMENAL

All born in this world,
One among the billion souls.
All bonds and people,
Growing with us old.

If you are the basic,
To pass the days faster.
To pass the tragic years.
And fears that mattered.

Love and fondness and
Madness for something.
Enough wildness,
To swim not to sink.

The more the sacrifice,
Out of the comfort zone.
For an unattainable price,
To escape from hell.

❧

The first death you saw,
With no sight.
The first life you held
A hand full of life.

❧

We all love animals,
We treat them well.
Being animals,
We often eat them well.

❧

Every last breath,
Of the last man in war.
His last thought could be,
That peace is a scar.

❧

It is all phenomenal.
We all die unaware
Of some facts and
Dreams that glared.

YiN & YaN

XLV

NOCTURNAL MIND

I have been up every night,
With short attempts to sleep.
Closing my eyes tight,
There is so much to seek.

❧

May be not tired enough but buzzed,
Not drenched with sweat and blood.
After trying every method,
Just fed up with being up.

❧

There is a love for the morning,
Awaiting since years.
Which my heart finds absconding,
And full of fears.

❧

But the dawn never met,
As soul leaves authority.
Carrying the promise so kept,
For meeting the reality.

NiGhTmArE

XLVI

DIVE IN YOUR CREATIONS

Drop your shoulders,
Be silent for a while.
Pervade your eyes,
And that hidden smile.

&

Segments you left behind,
Fondness and agony of ages.
Retard your emotions,
See if it amazes.

&

Read some stories,
Of dukes and beggars.
Personas of various kinds,
Oath makers and heart breakers.

Write poetries and phrases,
About mythical situations.
Something which embraces,
Your thoughts and visions.

Perform an act,
Depict tragic characters.
The one which lack,
Feelings and factors.

Create the colours,
From your own light,
Paint your canvas,
And paint right inside.

When there is a diversion,
On the only road.
Do Split yourself,
To walk on both.

Caste your world,
A world of oceans.
Empty your self,
Dive in your creations.

AsTrAl wAy

PeAce

XLVII
MADE OF COTTON

People are diverse and difficult,
Who all terrorize each other.
The ones out of the cult,
Out of the world from here.

They can paint you,
May spill theirs colours.
Took out the best of you,
Also the part worst of yours.

They can absorb the pain,
Also absorb the concerns.
They can fade the darkness,
Just like a cotton burns.

ShAdEs

XLVIII

A SUICIDAL LIVES

As I close my eyes,
There is something to see.
Deep down inside,
What it likes to be.

A skinny body looks dead,
Still alive maybe.
With hands on his head,
Who is seeking a key.

Pair of pale eyes,
Palpitations of the heart.
An ordinary pile of flesh,
With abandoned parts.

In all the remnant nights,
And in the wholeness of days.
There's a man that writes
For others to find ways.

ॐ

His skins veiling skins,
And unveiling mind.
He is an animal,
Escaped from the wild.

ॐ

Less troubled by life
More obsessed with death.
He is self-driven,
Struggling for the depth.

ॐ

ToUgH

XLIX

LOVE OR WAR

It's been too much of love from my side,
Because I can feel the fear so bad.
Bringing me up from the high skies,
In the real world I forget to had.

When did this happen, which moment,
What day It was, does not matter.
It's a spark and sparks untill frozen,
Till no hard feelings are left to shatter.

Nothing good before you came closer,
Knowing the fact, I'm different and weak.
Now I'm mostly shivering and sober,
And there is a lot to seek.

I know how to get everything alright,
With my rage,this war is yet to fight.
I killed that self, changed my psych,
Healed my self from this scar full of life.

❧

But It all goes on with the passing time,
And we have much time to spare.
Anything was sounding right,
Sadly none of my words got your ears.

❧

There is a mind full of concerns for you,
I expect no sympathy,just be true,
I have been up all night,morning is due,
No more words I write,
To show my love for you.

L
EASY AND HARD

To break all cages,
The trap we got on into.
To clear these stages,
To get back what life means to.

It is all easy
If you have the mindset.
To leave the misery,
Abandon the blind state.

It is hard and complex,
Takes a lot of courage
To accept what happened,
Without any regret.

No ReGrEts

LI

CHAOS

The one who is grinding
And silently mining himself.
To be of quality and joy,
With no one's help.

&

Some days we get,
Makes us feel the same.
Hardships and complications,
A heart full of shame.

&

No fine-dine,
No surprises to react.
It is the same fever,
Everytime so bad.

They all talk to much,
We never lied.
Each glare of them,
Revealed thier lies.

ThOuGhTs

LII

ABNORMAL

These are the miserable ones,
Paranoid and Insecure.
Who don't believe themselves,
Who keep wasting their cure.

The one keeps on thinking,
Scurtiny and surity of things.
Who sleeps while blinking,
Between reality and dreams.

Who run away from crowd,
Into the deep individual.
Who likes not to be liked,
Tangled in their own ritual.

If you can see more,
More like an optimistic.
You might not be abnormal,
You are simply artistic.

NoRmIe

LIII

MIND OF MINE

A revolution for peace,
For getting out of pain.
All of this within a bone,
That piece, as brain.

&

To diversify myself,
Into selves and more.
To fight with no help,
This selfless war.

&

There is hunger inside,
For Novels and knowledge.
To gain more conciousness,
More than the average.

When all this guilt,
Freezes every burning flame.
With the time which built,
Wounds from the shame.

૪૭

When labouring eyes,
Gets black and blocked.
The reflections of the light,
Carved tales and thoughts.

૪૭

The way to redemption,
Close to my heart.
Where the only obssesion,
Is to raise thy art.

૪૭

To read all around,
Many hidden frames.
To write what is found,
Not to be hailed.

૪૭

Mind of mine is a dagger,
Digging deep with no rest.
What is meant to be mattered,
Among the abnormal mess.

৵

ChOiCe

Pain can be resisted only when
The same act is not embraced again.

৵

ಚಿ

BaSe

ಚಿ

Not everyone holds the courage to seek the reality,
Though one stands with shields of tragedy.

ಚಿ

LaUgh

The more we hide from our real selves.
The less get to embrace the truth.